CONNIE NEWELL

Me, Myself and I Plus You:

A Simple Little How-To Clothes Story

First edition

This book was professionally typeset on Reedsy.
Find out more at reedsy.com

Contents

1

Introduction

Dressing, or simply putting clothes on, is a daily occurrence (well for most of us). Some people spend a great deal of time on it; others throw a pair of sweats on and are good to go. I go either way and it doesn't bother me a bit that I am not always in the current trendy style as I dress for my style and what makes me feel good. So what is this little book about? Adding in some quick and basic knowledge that will give you a bit of help with how you look and ultimately feel. You can go into so much more depth on this information and perhaps this little how-to book will pique your interest and you will take a deeper dive. If you do, I believe that it will only provide you with a broader understanding of the importance of color and style that anyone can obtain fairly easily. Looking good (or spectacular) but ultimately being comfortable is the ultimate compliment to yourself.

2

Color Me True

I remember doing my first "color" consultation and it was fun and probably helped me in my first go around although I enjoyed other colors outside of that color range and continued to buy. I was deemed a "Summer"; then about 10 years later, I found myself in Washington D.C. for work and some co-workers talked me into another consultation party and I was deemed a "Jewel Summer ". The difference between the two? Summer with its softer version of colors vs Jewel Summer with the bolder, jewel tone summer colors. At that particular time, I had more of the bolder, jewel tone colors in my closet so maybe my inner style fashionista must have known the difference before my logical mind put two and two together. Both these Summers were cool undertone colors. What does that mean? When it comes to color it means whether you are going to look like you have had a good 8 hours sleep or on the other hand, like death warmed over (not a good look on anyone). For the longest time, I never bought into it fully even though paying for two consultations must have checked off a strong underlying desire to know more. I never paid attention to "what" the colors were, just if I liked them. Who

knew that colors were all quite regimented; that a primary color or some say hue was that much different from a shade (hue/pure color + black added), or a tone (hue/pure color + gray added) or a tint (hue/primary color + white added). This is the simple version, you can find much more complex definitions of color out there but primary/hue colors are going to be your bolder true colors, the shade colors you are going to definitely see a black undertone (looks like it is dirty), tone colors look washed out with the gray added (think of those "old" barn woods that were in vogue for a while, either the gray color or the washed out red) and the tints you are always going to see the white undertone to the primary/hue. The primary/hue and the tone colors are slanted more towards the cool undertones while the shade and tint colors work out better for the warmer undertones. Just for fun and games, once you feel you know your undertone; find a color that you like (my sample color was red) and see if you can find the true primary, then one that looks dirty, one that looks grayed and one that has a white underlying tint. You can line them up and physically see the difference. Once you do that for the initial color you choose; practice by taking another color and doing the same and again and again until your eye can just quickly tell at a glance. This exercise will also help in choosing or confirming your undertone whether warm or cool and sometimes neutral (most people will fall into the warm or cool range).

Below are the color wheels for the main color categories; secondary colors have a range depending on how much of each of the two primaries are mixed. The colors in the secondary wheel below show equal amounts. If you were to take a different ratio, such as more yellow than blue you would have more of a yellow green color and vice versa more of a blue green color.

Primary (Hue) Colors

Primary and Secondary Colors

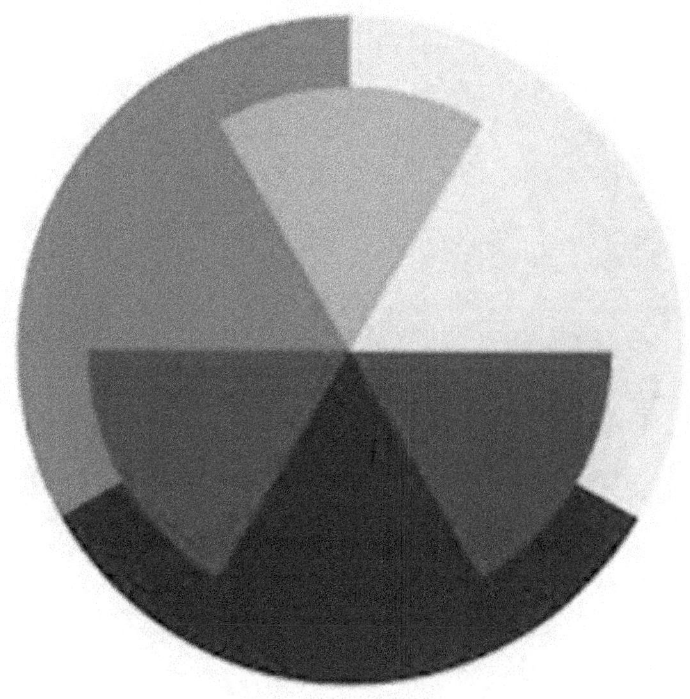

Primary, Secondary and Tertiary Colors

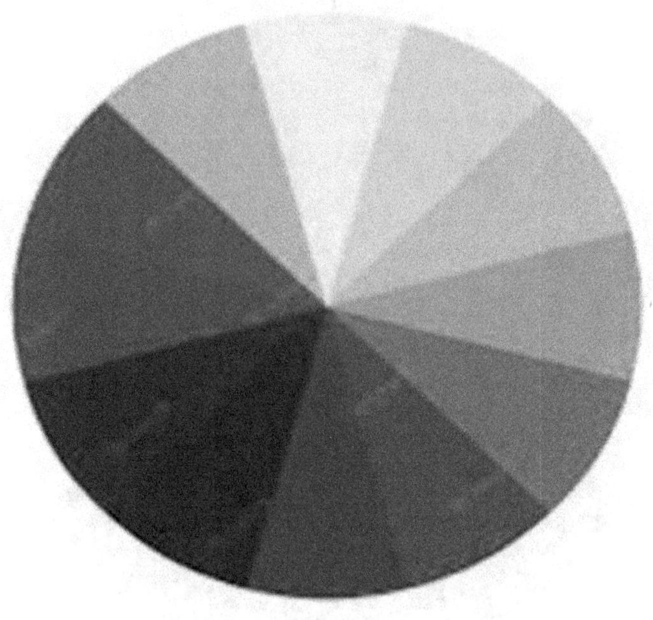

First, figure out whether you have cool, warm or neutral undertones. I know some people go into stores and have the sales personnel make recommendations or make up artists choose makeup for your skin tone and you can try that but please remember that every year has "in colors" that need to be sold. This year's red for example is a warm red (black/brown/rusty shades) so everywhere I go that is what I see and I can't wear it so if I am in dire need of something red this year, I might be shopping around quite a bit to find any wearable red for me. Are this year's colors yours? Great, stock up on basics as they may not come around again for a couple of years. But if not, look at your current

wardrobe and buy the least amount you can and if you have the time and fortitude, shop around.

Some simple ways to check your skin undertone:

First, let's clarify skin tone and skin undertone. Your skin tone can change due to external factors (tan, sunburn) but your skin undertone always remains the same. It is best if you can look at your skin with no makeup, hair pulled back away from face and in the best natural light possible.

Cool Undertone: Usually you can see the pink, red or bluish undertones in your skin. Cool undertone people tend to sunburn faster and you turn pink or red pretty quickly. If you require a lot of suntan lotion and still get pink/red quickly, you are most likely cool. A cool undertone sunburn will turn into a rosy/reddish or cinnamon colored tan. If you can see your veins in the wrist, elbow or any other place, and they are a bluish/purplish color, that shows the cooler side. You can also check to see whether silver or gold color jewelry compliments your skin with silver color being a better fit for cooler tones and yellow gold colors for the warmer tones. I personally wore yellow gold for years because I just didn't like the look of silver with my clothes. What does that tell you? I think I was wearing the wrong warmer color clothes so of course the silver didn't look quite right or didn't "fit" with the look. Once I started wearing silver (or platinum, white gold or stainless steel), with my correct cool colored clothes, I couldn't go back to wearing the yellow gold, it just didn't look or feel right. There really is a method to the madness. Another way to determine undertone is to take a piece of really white paper (think printer paper) and hold it up against your skin. Find a place with lots of natural bright

light to get the best comparison. If your skin looks pinkish against the bright white, you have a cool undertone.

Warm Undertone: Look for yellow, peach or gold undertones; olive skin will have yellow, green or golden undertone and sallow skin will have yellow or green undertones. When you go out in the sun, you may burn a tiny bit but nothing like the cooler tone people. Your tan will be peach, caramel, golden or even an olive tone (no rosy/reddish). Veins in your wrist, elbow or any other place will be greener rather than the cool blue. Warm tones look best in gold (yellow, rose, warm bronze, brass) jewelry. Try putting a gold-colored bracelet against a primary hue red and a rusty or black undertone red and you will definitely see the difference. It will clash with the primary hue red but complement the rusty or black undertone red. You can do the same thing with a piece of silver colored jewelry to just get the experience and feel of the difference. If you use the white paper test as noted above, your skin should look yellowish against the bright white confirming you have a warm undertone.

Neutral Undertone: To me, my original thought was thinking neutral would seem to be the easiest to work with and perhaps for some people it might be but it can be tricky and more work to figure out. I might try to check several colors and see which ones I feel the best or are the most comfortable in and seem to give my skin more of a glow. Don't assume that you will either be cool or warm undertone as the normal. If you are neutral then you have a mix of cool and warm undertones. For instance, using the bright white paper test, you may not notice a predominant skin shade (pink/yellow or even red/bluish/peach/gold), it may just look neutral with no real color, your skin tone and undertone may be

very close or the same color. If your skin looks gray (combination of yellow/green), you may have an olive type complexion with a neutral undertone. You may burn or tan equally well with no real defining reddish/peachy/caramel/ golden tan but more of a neutral color tan. I don't know if there are any statistics out there that give percentages of cool, warm and neutral but there seems to be more information on the cool and warm rather than the neutral so possibly neutral could be in the minority.

Draping has been used quite a bit to figure out undertones and if something you are interested in doing along with the above tips, then you will need a fairly substantial piece of cloth or clothing to cover the upper half of your body. You will need to find several colors and within those colors find the primary hue, same color with black undertones, same color with grayed undertones and same color with an underlying white tint. An easier way maybe would be to find a true basic black black, ivory white, neutral gray (no yellow/gold/purple/blue undertones) and a mustard color. You will drape these across your upper body. You can look in a mirror yourself but if you have someone who is objective/truthful to jot notes, that is even better. What you will be looking for with each color is:

If the color is correct for you, you should see the following:

- You see your face first, front and center, cloth is secondary (have you heard the saying you are wearing the dress vs the dress wearing you? Insert face for the dress and you will see what I mean – you want the face wearing you!)
- Your skin tone looks great like you have just had a spa treatment and glows with an inner light (skin is bright and

even looking)

- **You look younger (less lines, less shadows and dark circles don't show as much)**
- **Eyes are clear with brighter eye color**

If the color is NOT correct for you:

- **You see the cloth first so the cloth is dominant and face is seriously secondary**
- **Your face is secondary because it looks washed out or pale or in some cases it looks ruddy from the cloth undertones**
- **You will look older, harsher, tired or maybe even like you are sick**
- **Any skin imperfections will stand out or be much more noticeable: dark circles under eyes, wrinkles, blemishes, fine lines look deeper; skin looks like it needs a serious exfoliation, texture looks rougher**
- **Eyes are dull and eye color subdued**
- **Any perceived flaws will stand out like smaller eyes, longer, wider or larger nose, any feature that is asymmetrical to other features**

If you look the best with black or the neutral gray, you are a cool undertone. If you look best with the ivory white or the mustard, you are a warm undertone.

A quick note on "nude" colors. Nude means naked so these nudes are close to your skin color. This means you would follow the same rules as other colors as nude colors also have cool, warm or neutral undertones. Remember your skin tone can be any color from very fair to very dark but you will still need to use your

undertone for the correct nude for you. Your nudes can be all the way from an exact match to your skin tone to darker shades of the same skin tone depending on what you like, want or even for seasonal variances. Any nude must match your undertone or will clash with any other clothing you are wearing that contains your correct undertone. A yellow based nude top will look "off" with a cool black suit whereas a pink based nude top will look classic and chic. Same holds true for a warm brown suit and a pink undertone nude looking "off" whereas wearing the yellow based nude top will look classic and chic. If you are shopping and not really sure just by looking at the "nude", put it up against a warm color (mustard or color with a black undertone) and a cool color (primary hue cherry red or blue) and see which one complements or clashes with and you will know whether cool or warm.

3

Geometry and Looking GOOD

By geometry, I mean what is your body shape? There are five main body shapes: Pear, Inverted Triangle, Rectangle, Apple and Hourglass. Just like everything else in life, you most likely won't have the perfect fit into one of these shapes but you will have the basic identification rules. You may think you are one shape but if you follow the rules, you will figure out what you are even if you do have something in your shape that doesn't fit perfectly into the ideal rule. I am an Inverted Triangle which means my shoulders are wider than my hips, but when I gain weight it is in my stomach area which some would look at and casually say, oh you are an apple shape....but no, the rules for my particular shape apply to my entire body and not a temporary change in it. Your bust size can be varied for any shape, you don't have to have an hourglass figure to have an ample bust size.

You will need a good tape measure to take your measurements to identify what shape you are. Measure as follows:

SHOULDERS: Measure at the very top of where the arm meets

shoulder (if you go any higher, the tape measure will slip upwards off your body, any lower and you will not get a proper measurement) so this is a particular one and not easy to get. It was frustrating for me and I eventually needed someone to help hold the tape and keep it in a straight line across my back.

BUST: Wear a bra that brings your breasts up where you want them to look your best (no sports bras and no padded bras) and measure at the fullest part. Make sure the tape measure stays straight around the entire body at the same level. I was able to do this on my own because I had two perpendicular mirrors to check but if you feel that the tape measure is not staying straight all of the way around, do ask for help keeping it straight.

WAIST: Measure around the narrowest part of your middle section. If you have gained weight and it is in this area; do take the measurement but first utilize the shoulder and hip measurements and see what that gives you, then factor in the waist.

HIPS: Measure the fullest part below your hip bone but above the crotch. Again, if you have gained weight and it is accumulating in the hips, you can look at the shoulder and waist initially.

Reading the below characteristics of the shapes will also help you figure out your body shape using the above measurements as your baseline.

Pear: The key measurement is that the shoulders are narrower than the hips. Even though your shoulders are narrower than your hips, you can still have a full bust. You also may have a thinner waist and smaller hips just by looking at your body but the key

is in the measurement: shoulders are still narrower than the hip measurement.

Inverted Triangle: The key measurement for the inverted triangle is that the shoulders are wider than the hips by at least 5%. I didn't know that is what I was called but I knew that it was better for me to buy separates because I was always at least 2 sizes smaller in pants and skirts than in jackets and other tops. I am fairly average in bust size but an inverted triangle can be busty and fuller in the midsection with a bigger bottom also but follow the key 5% measurement to decide.

Apple: The key measurement for the apple shape is your bust; it will be your largest measurement. Shoulders and waist are wider than your hips. Your torso makes a v-shape similar to an inverted triangle but you will have a wider waist.

Rectangle: The key measurements for this body shape are that your shoulder and hip measurements are about the same and your waist is LESS than 25% smaller. You can have an ample bust, a bigger bottom and a waistline closer to the maximum of 25% but the measurements rule.

Hourglass: The key measurement for the hourglass figure is that your bust/shoulder measurements are within half an inch of your hips and your waist is very defined. You look like an hourglass!

It doesn't matter which body shape you are; each of the shapes have their pluses and minuses and everyone identifies those differently and no one is wrong. I want thin arms but alas, probably not going to happen. You have lived with your body a long time but actually putting a name and characteristics to it allows you to see what you 'think" those pluses and minuses are and dress accordingly to highlight all those beautiful features you love and minimize those that you aren't too fond of. Bottomline, you are going to want to dress to accent those features you adore and minimize those you don't. Great legs? Show them off! A nice bust? Show it off! A nice rounded bottom? Yes, show it off! Brighter colors and patterns highlight; solid neutrals or less bright colors are for those areas you don't want to highlight. All of you have colors as shown in Chapter 1 that are your colors; work with them to get the effect you want.

4

Am I What? Or What? Or What?

This chapter will touch on your style, current and what you might want to change or items you want to incorporate into your everyday or evening attire. Some women go for just one basic style, others like to change it up all the time with pieces of clothing or accents or maybe only for special occasions, whether subtly, a somewhat noticeable change or change the entire look all over. You can do it any way you want and it will depend on what you are comfortable with. I would recommend making changes with items that you aren't spending a fortune on and that you can remove quickly if after a couple of hours, you are done with it and know that it is not you. You tried it, good for you, now go on to the next item(s) you think you might like to try to change up your dressing style. You will eventually find those items that make you smile and feel beautiful.

Below are some general style types that you can use as a baseline. You should try to figure out that baseline so you can purchase or clean out your current closet to reflect that style and then add to it with pieces that you love and fall into that category, you love

and will use to spice up your everyday look or spectacular OMG pieces that will let you rule the room. I have found that if I have to find something I need for a look, I don't have as much luck as if I am out and about and if I have time, taking 30 minutes to an hour and just browsing. You don't need as much time to browse if you know all your colors as it will be easier to just shop those colors. If you have a basic outfit style, that will also help in time allotted so you can spend a bit more time looking for something that you think you might want that will give your outfits a little pizazz or upswing, like anything with a pop of color or a pair of earrings that are just a little "more" than your usual ones, or a beautiful purse that will make some of your outfits look spectacular, a pair of shoes that will make your whole outfit stand out, or even a snazzy belt or scarf. You get the idea. You can also keep a running list like I do where I jot down items that are either basics I need (just wore out my last black tank top that I wear under everything) or my red flats thar are on their last legs and I wear them for a pop of color with an all-black look (or maybe I will change it up and replace them with a great purple or royal blue if I can't find any red ones I like), or maybe you saw something on someone else and you thought that is me so put it on your list. I have actually gone up to women several times and complimented them and asked if they would mind telling me where they got that piece as it is so gorgeous, all except one have been more than happy to help out.

Minimalist Classic Style: **I have heard this style also called chic and sophisticated which is totally applicable as this type of style tends to be timeless with its structured tailoring, high quality fabrics and construction, both solid and neutral colors for the most part (for me a houndstooth is classical timeless so I will always have one or more items of that), bold colors, and a**

monochromatic or high contrast color look. Your neutral colors can have pops of color but only to accent. Same with any patterns, stick with simple one or two colors that support or accent the overall timeless look and do not mix different patterns together. I am this type and I actually do have some old, old clothes that I keep on wearing because the style has never gone away. I have coats, jackets, skirts, jeans, long sleeve white silk blouses, purses and even a couple pairs of shoes. I like to think that since I spent serious money on them at the time, I am getting my money's worth! I will spend money on something that has the timeless tailored lines and details because I know it will last for years. I will not usually spend money on something trendy that might last a few weeks or a season at most, although I will admit to making a few regrettable mistakes over the years. This, of course, is up to you but do stop and really think about how you would use it and if it fits your overall minimalist style or will support it well. The minimal classic look can seem dull, uninteresting or even boring to some but those who wear it depend on the look to support both their serious, analytical side and their fuss-free nature. All of their clothes are easily coordinated with little effort and they can up their game easily with the small details like a metallic belt, bold colored shoe and/or purse, jewelry, tailored scarf or even a hat. You can also add in small details from any of the below styles to add some uniqueness to your simpler no-fuss style. I happen to like a few Edgy and Cute style items and do incorporate them as accents.

Soft Classic Style: You are more comfortable in neutral or calming colors like green, blue, purple and navy. Black can be overpowering if too much in the outfit; better to have it as an accent to more neutral colors. You can also utilize another darker

neutral as your "black". Bold and intense colors and styles can be overwhelming; you need subtle and simple with less rather than more details. Soft Classic needs touchable fabrics like soft knits, velvet, silk, cashmere, chiffon, shearling that evoke comfort. You won't like any clothes with fabrics that are scratchy, itchy, stiff, uncomfortable or restrictive (too tight). Your solid colors will be softer and more subtle (more neutrals and soothing colors). Prints will be smaller and colors can be bolder but edges will be softer to blend in with the other colors. Florals will also be softer rather than bold and will also have edges that blend in more subtly to the other colors. Ruffles will be softer rather than structured and not overly large. Lace will be soft (and not itchy) and design will look more romantic than structured. Rather than squared off bottoms to jackets, vests and other tops, you will prefer rounded softer hems; skirt hems may be soft and wavy. You may prefer shawl collars on jackets and sweaters. Another preference or comfort level may be more length in your tops or skirts; some structure will still look and feel better like a straight maxi, a longer structured straight cut jacket or sweater or a tailored tunic top. The softer more subtle details will differentiate the Soft Classic vs the Minimalist Classic style.

Edgy Classic Style: A few things that add edgy to your Edgy Classic style are leather or leather trim, angular patterns (especially triangular shaped), v-necklines, asymmetrical lines, exposed, zippers, studs, cut-outs, more texture, ripped fabric and animal prints. I always think biker chic but to be Edgy Classic these items would not be your whole look but more accents (major or minor) or one or two max edgier pieces of clothing. Moto jackets come to mind for an edgy look but you don't have to go full moto; you can have a softer lighter leather with a classical cut with the

angled zippers in the body and zippers on the sleeves. I happen to have two colored moto jackets so style is edgy but not quite as much as a black version. You can wear a crew neck wool black sweater with a pair of ripped jeans (maybe only one small rip to multiple larger rips) with a pair of classical black flats/loafers. A leather skirt or leather pants is edgy (and a large piece) so keep everything else towards the classic or maybe one smaller accent. Leather trim on clothes is another way to add leather as an edgy accent. You can replace buttons on a blouse, dress or sweater with an exposed zipper. You can have a few studs on a jacket, coat or a pair of black flats/loafers with straight leg pants and a classic blouse/sweater. Jewelry can be quite edgy with very sharp angles or points or triangles with an otherwise totally minimal classical look. Wearing a faux black fur vest or jacket over classical jeans/pants with sweater and black low-heeled booties can be called edgy especially if trimmed in leather or having other edgy accents. An animal print blouse adds an edge to a pair of tailored pants with high heels or booties. I don't think it takes more than a few of the edgy items to provide an Edgy Classic look so be careful of overdoing it unless you want total Edgy vs Edgy Classic.

Sporty Classic Style: Sporty Classic does not mean you are necessarily heading for the gym. It is a more casual look that is comfortable but still put together, functional and chic. This is an always on the go type of style and clothes need to be simple, practical and easy because so many other things need to get done in the time you have, but it does not mean sloppy or that you don't want to look great. Layering is a good option because it is functional, practical and easy on and off during the day. Denim, leather and very slim silhouette puffer vests (try to keep away from bulky look) and same material type jackets are easy to layer

over t-shirts, sweaters, sweatshirts or even flannel shirts to give you a sporty look. Stylish slim-fit hoodies are also good, a quick throw on either by themselves or you can layer with a slim vest although keep from looking bulky or sloppy. Hats are great for bad hair days or you just want to add a bit more to your outfit. They can be baseball, newspaper boy, beanies, berets, whatever you have on hand that feels comfortable and can match your colors or you can bring in a pop of color with them. Since you are on the go with all kinds of activities your best choice pants are: jeans, jogger style, cargo, leggings and chinos. These will all work well and will be comfortable especially if you can get them with a little stretch in them. They will also still look good at the end of your busy day. If you prefer dressier pants/trousers or skirts, also make sure they have some stretch to help keep you comfortable in your activities and still be functional. Tops can be t-shirts, button ups, henleys, sweaters and should include pockets, anything that hints at sports or athletics (but is not workout clothing), graphics that look more sporty casual, a stripe down a long sleeve shirt or jacket or other details that would make you think of an athletic uniform. Materials that are good for sport casual wear are denim, knits, t-shirt, chambray and natural fabrics like cotton, linen, wool, cashmere. It would be better if you did not choose clothes that require dry cleaning or are high maintenance, you will most likely not end up wearing them because they will take too much time and effort to maintain. Sports leisure has come into its own, so sneakers, boots of all kinds, boat shoes, slip-ons, Converse and stylish running shoes are all good choices.

Cute Classic Style: This style is more upbeat looking with its brighter lighter colors and more patterns or multi details. You will want to keep your colors fresher and fun. Cute Classic will wear

lighter weight fabrics like thin crepe, knits, linen, chiffon and softer cottons that are not as structured or bulky. Don't let your clothes weigh you down; balance is key, not too lightweight nor too bulky, lean more to the lighter side rather than the heavier side. You want lightness. Rather than solids, you are going to be drawn to more crisp florals/fruit patterns, and you can mix patterns to have a busier look or a more patterned look (mix florals with stripes). You will need to decide how busy and how large the patterns are but most of the time it will be medium to smaller patterns. Cute Classic also includes hearts, polka dots and circles. I use polka dots to incorporate into my minimalist classic. I love cardigans with bigger polka dots and t-shirts with smaller polka dots. You want to keep your classical style with the cute so don't go overboard with every piece having a heart, circle or polka dots. These should be more accent to give your classical look a cute twist. You can wear jewelry to bring in hearts and circles into play as a cute accent. I happen to love a little bling and you can bring that into your Cute classic with smaller accents: jewelry, belt, shoe accents, headband, crystal buttons to name a few. Patent leather in shoes or purses is also a wonderful accent especially in the brighter colors. Most animal prints are not associated with cute, but you can try a small zebra print or even a white leopard or cheetah print especially if the print itself looks more like a polka dot or circle (you might have to search a bit for this but it would make a unique accent in a blouse or light vest or sweatshirt).

5

Painting My Face

Makeup is a huge area to cover and could take an entire book so I will just provide some overall tips to help coordinate your face look with your overall look.

Your skin tone can change with external factors, such as getting a tan but your skin undertone always remains the same: cool, warm or neutral. Looking at someone else, you might have the same or very similar skin tone but have a different skin undertone.

I look far better in the cool undertones for clothes and most make-up but in certain brands I seem to have better luck with neutral foundation undertone shades. Always try several of what your undertone is plus a neutral or too just to make sure. You can blend your makeup into your neckline but it is best if you can find the best actual exact match to your skin. Don't automatically look to family or friends either for their makeup colors even if they do look like they are the same skin tone as you. I have four sisters and all of us have different skin tones, all the way from porcelain to more of an olive/sallow. All of us, but one, seem to have the same

undertone but quite different shades. You are unique to yourself so spend the time to find your perfect shade(s), it will be worth it and save you time and product trying to fix an incorrect one.

Makeup colors for both eyeshadow, blush and lip color should follow your skin undertone and clothes undertone. Unlike the face makeup, these colors are more noticeable and you do not want them clashing with your clothes colors as your overall look will be off or unbalanced. You can use more color on your face the bolder your clothes color choices are and reverse if you are wearing subdued colors to balance your overall look. Not every color on your face needs to be bold but not all should be subdued either; practice a little to see where your balance is. Always think of a balance between the two.

Minimalist Classic: It is best to keep your makeup simple (minimal) and classy. You may not like to wear too much makeup (I don't) but you should define your eyebrows and lips (whether a bold color or a darker neutral that defines the lip (so you can at least see it). I don't like taking mascara off at the end of the day but I have to admit it opens up the eyes and with those three, your face will look quite nice.

Soft Classic Style: As the style indicates, this is a softer, more subtle look. You may not want to wear much or any makeup but you do need some framework to balance your clothes. Keep it simple with soft eyebrows, softer mascara colors (Navy, Purple, Charcoal for cooler tones and Brown if you are warm undertones). A soft smokey eye can be a simple and elegant look. Depending on how bold or subtle your clothes colors are will help decide your lip color along with how deep/dark you make your smokey eye.

Edgy Classic Style: Depending on how edgy your clothes are will determine your makeup. You can add a bit more eyeliner and smudge it for a smokier look but don't make the whole eye look dark/black. A little blush will go a long way and a bolder lip color will balance with the edgier look if you are comfortable with the color. You don't have to do red if it's too bold, maybe a bolder pink would be better. The Edgy Classic look can be more overwhelming so ensure your face still takes center stage and maintain the balance between the two.

Sporty Classic Style: Because you are on the go so much and like simple, you won't want to deal with putting on a lot of makeup let alone worry about it all disappearing throughout the day. Eyebrows and waterproof mascara for the eyes and tinted (as bold as you feel comfortable with to give your face some color) lip balm that you can quickly re-apply during the day would be your best option. If I have time in the morning, I will use a lip pencil all over my lip for color and then use the lip balm over it when I think about it during the day.

Cute Classic Style: Makeup for you will follow your clothes traits: light, fresh and bright. No heavy makeup for you; everything will have a light touch for a glowing face. You will also like it simple and easy to do; you have much more fun things to do than put on makeup!

6

Summary

I have two resources that I have settled on over the past few years that I believe provide me with what I need to look and feel good, using colors that support me and also styles that support both my body type and the type of person I am (or in some cases the one I want to be). I don't get anything from these references other than "paying forward" if you would like to check either or both out. AND, if you do, then pay it forward to other people who you think might benefit. We can all use some help or a starting point in this area sometimes and this is a nice way to do that for others. Both are also noted in the references below.

Carol Tuttle @ Dressing Your Truth

This site was primarily for women but is now including men which I think is great (they want to look good and feel great too even if they won't truly admit it). This is a slightly different slant on utilizing color and due mainly to her background which I found resonated quite strongly with me. There is a free resource on the site that provides your "type" and you can go from there

if you wish. If you delve deeper into her offerings, you will find great support and ample opportunities to ask questions whether on their daily/weekly/monthly communications. Carol herself is very down to earth and very much emphasizes using the information for not only support but making the information your own.

Stunning Society

This site only provides information for women but is a fun site with lots of everyday support with what to wear as you are learning all of the basics. This site goes into not only colors but in-depth information on body types, types of materials (I personally learned a great deal in his area that I had not paid much attention to before), patterns, texture, shoes, jewelry and more. She has a Facebook page that she does videos on and if you want more, she breaks out your style and has different programs for those also. I do believe you really get your money's worth if you go that route. I certainly feel I have.

Both of these sites are ongoing that provide you weekly, monthly and sometimes daily information/support so you are not left hanging with what is next. You can do as much or as little as you want, your choice.

I agree with the philosophy that once you believe you have figured out the basics then do start to rely on your intuition or how you feel in what you are wearing. I remember hearing don't buy something if it does not fit your criteria for color, style etc. even if it is on sale for $5 or it is a "really good deal" because you will probably never pull it out of your closet to wear if it does not feel right or uncomfortable in any way when you put it on. So even

if it was on sale or the "best ever deal", it doesn't do any good in your closet if you intuitively know it is not for you. You will get to the point of trusting yourself and not others on what is right for you so you will know when it doesn't feel right in some way or all ways and you will feel uncomfortable wearing it; trust those hard-won instincts! Another tip I learned was: what do people say when they see you? If they say, what a gorgeous top or skirt or dress, what are they seeing? Your clothes, not you. But if they say, you look great or gorgeous today, they are seeing the whole you which means you are spot on, give yourself a high five!! Keep in the back of your mind what were the elements of those clothes: color, style/design, material, etc and keep notes so you can start to replicate similar looks until it becomes second nature to just put it all together easily and effortlessly. All of this helps too when you shop because you know what colors and styles you want and that narrows choices and the time required to shop down considerably. A win-win for all of it!

Good Luck and enjoy feeling good about how you look and feel. Take all the tips and make them your own style that is all you! Have fun! Smile because you LOOK gooooood!!

7

References

Tuttle, C. (n.d.). *What Is Dressing Your Truth*. LiveYourTruth.Com. Retrieved August 21, 2022, from https://my.liveyourtruth.com/dyt/what-is-dressing-your-truth/

Grow, A. (n.d.). *Stunning Style*. StunningStyle.Com. Retrieved August 21, 2022, from https://stunningstyle.com/

www.ingramcontent.com/pod-product-compliance
Lightning Source LLC
LaVergne TN
LVHW052113160826
845678LV00015B/3520

* 9 7 9 8 8 4 8 4 0 0 2 9 8 *